Tales from the Phone Room

A Look Back at the "Golden Age" of Telemarketing

By
Mike Straka

Tales From the Phone Room: A Look Back at the "Golden Age" of Telemarketing

Copyright 2014 by Mike Straka

ISBN 978-1519249999

Second edition

For Roberta, my number one fan.

Contents

Foreword

Early in 2009, my wife Roberta suggested that, after hearing me tell these stories for over ten years, I should write them down. I, of course, followed her advice because a successful husband should always follow his wife's advice. Several months later, she urged me to submit one of the stories to *Bandwagon,* a bi-monthly publication that is published by the Circus Historical Society. I honestly did not believe that the folks there would find any merit in my stories. However, Roberta proved me wrong again.

Starting with the 2009 May-June issue, many of the stories that appear here were published with the support of the *Bandwagon* editor, Mr. Fred D. Pfening III. In addition, that support was continued when Mr. Fred Pfening Jr. took over as editor. I also wish to acknowledge the kind support of John and Mardi Wells, the editors of the Circus Fans of America's publication, *The White Tops,* who published some of these stories as well. For this book I have added just a bit more detail because many of the *Bandwagon* and *White Tops* readers already had a basic understanding of the phone business.

I would like to thank Tom Ogden and Paula Grande for their immense help in the editing process, and I would also like to extend my great appreciation to E. C. Streeter, an old friend from my days on Circus Kirk, for contributing the afterword.

Mike Straka
Pocono Mountains
March 2015

Introduction

It happens all too often. You're just getting ready to eat dinner and the phone rings. Before you check the caller I.D., you pick up the receiver. That's when the pitch begins. Perhaps they are selling home improvements, lower rates on your credit card or an all-expenses-paid vacation to Dakota, Nebraska. Maybe the pleasant voice on the phone would like you to buy some tickets to help a few underprivileged kids go to a circus. We have all experienced this at one time or another.

With the advent of call screening, the do-not-call lists, and caller I.D., we receive a lot fewer unwanted sales calls these days. Before all of the modern technology and phone laws, though, there was a golden age of phone solicitation, and for twenty years from 1978 to 1998 I played a small part in that memorable era.

During those decades, I was the road manager for a show that was part of the second largest entertainment phone operation in America. It was called "The World of Fantasy Players," a touring show that featured magic, circus acts and a cast of actors. We toured from Maine to California and presented the show as a fund raiser for local fraternal and civic clubs. And yes, the tickets for the show were sold through phone rooms.

I thus had a front row seat for some of the

humorous and occasionally outrageous antics of our merry band of promoters.

Before we get to the stories, it might be helpful to get to know the key people and a little about the mechanics of the operation. The show was created and produced by Phillip Morris, the owner and operator of Morris Costumes in Charlotte, North Carolina. He also produced touring theatrical shows and circuses. Often mistaken for being somehow associated with the tobacco company, Phil used to joke that his brother was Chester Fields!

The show was promoted by William English. Bill, as he was known to absolutely everyone, was a Harvard graduate who somehow ended up in this particular niche of show business. He oversaw the booking and promotion for every one of cities that we would perform in every year.

Each town was assigned a local promoter. His or, in a few cases, her job entailed setting up the phone room, which was simply an office or motel room with at least three phone lines. If this was our first time playing the town, the promoter would also "card" the town, a task that involved creating 3x5 index cards with a listing for each business and residence for the entire phone book. This was the pre-computer era, so you can imagine the amount of work this required. Known as "tap cards," these were crucial to the operation because they were where the information would be recorded as to whether the person being called agreed to buy any tickets. The promoter would then hire local sales people or use their own teams to sell the tickets. They collected all the money and turned it over to our show's local sponsor. In addition to overseeing the phone room, the promoter's obligations also included keeping things generally in line, this last duty being, as I found, a good bit easier said than done.

As for the phone men – again, most were men, but on occasion I ran across women – they were itinerant individuals who would either travel with a promoter or drift from phone room to phone room.

So there's our cast of characters. But before going on, let me state for the record that I have never let my memory get in the way of a good story.

So let me tell you a few tales.

"Heel and Toe" Man

This tale centers on an old time promoter named M.E. Van Dorstan. A gifted phone promoter, he traveled the country promoting our show and also spent many years running circus phone rooms. He worked fifteen to twenty cities each year for us. When I joined the show he was starting to slow down because he was getting old. He would joke that he was present when Alexander Graham Bell made his first call to Mr. Watson; he said he made the second call and tried to sell Watson some circus tickets.

He was a dead-ringer for Colonel Sanders of Kentucky Fried Chicken fame. On many occasions, he would even turn up at the show decked out in an all-white suit. He liked to be called Van. We never managed to find out what the M. or the E. stood for.

He had a young girlfriend named Amanda, who was an ex-hippie from the 1960s. I believe she was in her thirties, much younger than Van who was clearly twice that age. They had a large poodle named Poncho Villa, and they all traveled in Van's pride and joy: a 1962 pop-top Cadillac. He once explained that he had paid cash for it after a particularly successful promotion. Nothing took priority over that car. If Amanda wanted a new pair of shoes, she could wait. If the Cadillac needed new tires, then only the best would do.

I quickly figured out that the amount of ticket sales that Van would report to the sponsor was directly related to the mechanical well-being of his car. When we met up on show day, I would always start the conversation with an update on the Cadillac. If the repairs were minor, the gross ticket sales would be good. If, God forbid, something major happened, the gross would invariably suffer.

When we played Morehead City, North Carolina, Van told me he had to replace the entire engine! After seventeen years, he had driven an impressive 300,000 miles. As he related the matter, you would think that he had received a heart transplant. He personally oversaw the mechanics, even though he knew almost nothing about engines. Amazingly, the gross sales dropped $2,500 from the previous year. At some point in one of our conversations, Van mentioned that the new engine had run him about $2,500. Go figure.

In general, though, Van turned in impressive sales figures. So, to my mind, keeping the Cadillac running was just a part of the cost of doing business. He always seemed to get every last dollar out of every town he worked, and one key to his success was that he had a secret weapon that he used at the end of each promotion. Thanks to his many years in the business, he was familiar with the old "heel and toe" guys and was shrewd enough to borrow and then update one of their techniques.

Just before the show arrived in town and the phoning had all been done, Van would go over all the tap cards. As mentioned earlier, these were index cards with the name of the business, the business owner's name, and a record of previous purchases by that business. Of course, not everyone would say yes to the phone man's pitch. If the merchant refused to buy any tickets, the promoter would mark the tap card with a big "T.D." for "Turned Down." Van would then select thirty to forty T.D. cards and head out. He would pull up in his bright shiny Caddy and stroll into the business. He would introduce himself and ask to see Mr. Jones, the owner. He would tell the owner that the Rotary Club (or whatever sponsor we had) was finishing up their fund-raising campaign. He would then pull out the tap card and mention he had noticed that Mr. Jones had not purchased tickets for the show.

At this point, Van would simply shut up. He told me that a full 50 percent of the time the merchant would hem and haw but go ahead and make a donation. The other half would hold their ground and say they couldn't help. Van would then smile and say, "Well, I need to note this." He would then take the tap card and start writing on it, adding, "The club members wanted a list of everyone that said no." This was gutsy stuff, but it paid off. Almost every merchant caved in at that point.

Van's heel and toe work usually added more than $1,000 to each city. As I said, he was a gifted promoter.

The Wichita Lineman

Jim Fletcher was a big man, a good six feet five inches. He resembled Daddy Warbucks, bald head and all. He said that at one time he had been an account executive for Proctor & Gamble back in the early 1950s. He also claimed that his annual expense account was more than $20,000. I should note, however, that I obtained all this information after a long night of drinking Drambuie and beer shots, and I don't suppose I need to also note that such evenings were most definitely not a part of the expense account that Bill English provided his phone promoters!

In any event, Jim was also another one of our star phone promoters. The local sponsors just loved big old Jim, and this was all the more amazing because the local sponsor only received 20 percent on the tickets that Jim sold. Even though the point was always made to the sponsors that they would receive a full 50 percent of every ticket sold by their members, they never managed to peddle many tickets this way. But his good-humored charm always managed to soothe any concerns the sponsors might have had about this particular form of income disparity.

In addition to being personable, Jim was also ingenious, no more so than during our 1980 tour when we were scheduled to play Wichita,

Kansas. Our local sponsor was the Humane Society, and Jim was assigned the date. The problem was that after the first few days of work he realized that he was calling merchants and households that had been recently contacted by four other local sponsors.

Normally, a phone room would be opened by the promoter about four weeks prior to the show's arrival. Some phone rooms, however, remained open throughout the year. After they finished up with one sponsor, they would call the same merchants for another sponsor. To make matters worse, the local police had just sponsored a circus. When you get a call to help the police send some deserving kids to the circus, well it's hard to say no. It's not that people didn't care about the work of the Humane Society but, this was the fifth call within something like a week's time. Jim protested this assignment to Bill English. He wanted no part of this town and no part of this sponsor.

By the end of that first week he had only sold about $500 worth of tickets. He was now furious, but at the same time he was also determined to turn this promotion into a winner. He needed to because his paycheck depended on it. All of the promoters worked on a percentage of the gross sales. They received 30 percent of the ticket sales and had to pay their phone people out of that 30 percent. Jim had so far made a whopping $150 for a whole week of work. When he subtracted what he paid his people, then Wichita was not looking too good. The only other possible income he could hope for was the override. This was an additional 10 percent of sales that was collected by the show and kicked back to the promoter after the date was concluded. Of course, any outstanding debts, long distance phone charges or bar bills left by the promoter would be deducted from the override, and if his team didn't sell many tickets, then he was facing the prospect of a pretty skimpy override at best.

When I spoke with Jim and heard him describe his dismal situation, I mumbled something about doing the best he could, but in my mind, I wrote off Wichita and figured it would be a losing date.

When we arrived in Wichita three weeks later, Jim showed up at the theater with a big grin on his face. He then handed me the final sales recap sheet and said in his booming voice, "Read it and weep!"

My reaction was something like a jaw drop, followed by a muttered "What the hell?" Jim had sold $10,500 worth of tickets. Our normal sales were around $3,500.

It seems that Jim had concocted a sales pitch that was nothing short of brilliant. After that first week, he went down to the animal shelter and tape recorded hours of dogs barking and yelping. The next day he started his first call with the tape playing in the phone room. During the pitch, he would stop and say, "Oh no, they're putting another one down! You've got to help these animals." The sales, needless to say, rolled in.

It proved hard to turn down the Wichita lineman.

Where's the Elephant?

Before the phone promoters could start their work, a sponsor had to be found and the date booked. One of our best booking agents was Jackie Wilcox. Her job was to travel the country and sign up potential sponsors for our show. She lived in Hot Springs, Arkansas, and had a long and varied career in this business. I first met her in 1978 when our show played Hot Springs. Within ten minutes she had me convinced that I should join the Showman's Association. She said they had a wonderful club that I could visit any time I was in town. I think I mentioned to her that I lived in Pennsylvania, but Jackie was never one to take no for an answer. Her closing argument centered on how the association would bury me if I died on the road. This was strangely comforting to me. I continued my membership for many years, and I could see why Bill English wanted her on his team.

During that time, Bill was also booking the King Brothers and Sells & Gray circuses while also maintaining our route, and he often used the same promoters and agents for more than one show. Jackie might book one of the circuses for a summer appearance and find another sponsor in the town for our show later in the year.

This particular incident occurred in Ruston,

Louisiana. We were presenting "Snow White and Her Seven Magical Dwarfs" that year. As we drove into the civic center parking lot, I saw a committee of men in suits. They turned out to be the members of the sponsoring club. It's important to note here that our entire show moved in two vehicles. We had an 18-foot straight truck and one passenger van.

The committee chairman introduced everyone and then, looking at the truck, said, "You got the elephant in there?" I thought it was a joke, but as he went on, I quickly figured out that Jackie had mixed up the dates. She'd promised them a circus with elephants and the like. Without missing a beat I smiled and said that the rest of the show would be along shortly.

There were several ways I could have handled this (honesty comes to mind), but then again, I never seem to do things the easy way. What I did do was to make a quick change in the show. Just by sheer chance, we had an elephant costume on the show that one of the performers wore in a scene in the second half of the show. It was pink and very cute. I then strategically moved this character to the opening number in the show.

I did this because I knew that the sponsors had to be in the lobby selling tickets during the first part of the show. Just before the intermission, I noticed some of the committee members walking down the aisle. I approached them and said, "You're late! What's the matter? Couldn't you find the show? You missed the elephant. You should have seen him. The trouble it takes to train him, and you go and miss him. He was great. It was the best!" For some reason the fact that the creature I was referring to was distinctly more homo sapiens than pachyderm didn't seem to be impacting too heavily on my sense of honesty at that particular point in time.

After the show, not one member of the club asked me about the elephant. They all agreed that the show was wonderful for the kids, and they loved the circus acts we had on the show. We always managed to work traditional circus acts into the story line. During the grand ballroom scene in Snow White, for example, several acts were presented to amuse the King.

When I next caught up with Jackie I mentioned my dilemma and chided her about the fix she'd put me in. She immediately let out a laugh and said. "Oh, Mike it's all the same. Magic, circus, dwarfs—who can tell the difference!" And when I thought about it, I realized she was absolutely right. What difference was there? We were there to entertain. She had to have been close to seventy by then and had been around the block a lot more times than I had.

And it was just like Jackie to include dwarfs in her entertainment list.

Fun Phone Fact:
The American Public Communications Council reports that there are fewer than 500,000 payphones left in America. In 1995 the United States had 2.6 million payphones in service.

Interesting Venues

Every showman has a collection of memorably rough venues that they've worked, and I'm no exception. So I'll share a few.

We were scheduled to play the high school in Kenova, West Virginia, and as was often the case, we had no other details about the venue. This misadventure occurred in the late 1970s and was well before the days of Mapquest. We had to find the venue by asking around. The police were the best, followed by firefighters, but I never ruled out the bum on the corner. Hey, they do a lot of walking and know the streets.

This time it was the manager of the hotel where we were staying who was able to help us get to the high school we were booked into. The first thing he wanted to know was which high school we were looking for. It seems Kenova had two, but he knew where each one was and successfully directed us to the one that I had an address for.

As we pulled up to the building we could see that it was closed, but on closer inspection, it was apparent that the school had been closed for a good number of years. In fact, it had been condemned. The committee eventually showed up and said yes, this really was where the show would be held. I asked if the building had power. They told me that it had been turned off long ago, but not to worry, they had a generator and would run it to supply the power. They set up work lights around the auditorium, the kind they sell at the big box hardware stores. They also had two of them to put on the front of the stage to act as our stage lights. During the set-up, pieces of plaster fell from the ceiling onto the stage. The place was falling down around us! Fortunately, gravity was kind to us during the show, but I can't imagine the performance came off very well. Still, the audience seemed to like it, and the committee was happy that they had saved a few bucks.

On several occasions, we had to take extraordinary measures to present the show. In Mason City, Iowa, we arrived at the school and found it to be locked tight. Our appearance was during the summer, so no one was around. I'd called the sponsor two weeks prior and asked them to make sure someone with the school would be there to meet us on show day. When we found that we couldn't get in, I made several frantic phone calls to the sponsor but could not reach anyone.

Since we couldn't just sit there waiting for someone to show up, I walked around the school and checked the doors, but to no avail. I did notice, though, that one of the classroom windows had a large crack in it. I figured that they would be replacing it anyway... and so we "opened" it. I then asked my levitation assistant, Roberta, who also happened to be the smallest person in the troupe, to crawl inside. In as authoritative a tone as I could muster under the circumstances, I explained that she would not be breaking the law. Somehow she accepted this, and we shoved her through the window.

Thanks to Roberta we were able to load in and get the show ready on schedule. When the custodian finally arrived he seemed a little bent out of shape and demanded to know how we got into the building. So, with a straight face, I told him that the front doors were unlocked — technically, a true statement, I should point out. I'm not sure that he fully bought this explanation, but it was the only one I could manage to offer.

It turned out that the sponsors had planned all along for someone to open the school at that time, figuring that we really didn't need two whole hours to set up the show. Besides, it would have cost them a whopping $8.00 an hour extra for the custodian to arrive earlier.

As Oliver Hardy used to say to Stan Laurel, Midland, Texas, was another fine mess. Our sponsor was a local fraternal organization, and we were set to perform in the banquet room of their building. The club manager showed us where to park our trucks, and as we entered the building he said, "Don't look."

About a half hour before our arrival, Midland experienced an old fashion gully washer; it rained like nobody's business. Fortunately the rain had stopped by load-in time, but only outside the club, that is. Inside the club, it was still pouring rain! The club building had a flat roof, which had many holes. The club members had put down a flotilla of buckets and trash cans to catch the rain, and the manager assured me that it would stop "raining" by show time. I don't think he would have made a good weatherman. As things turned out, his forecast was off by about three hours.

The ceiling was still precipitating when we started the show, and as I stepped onto the stage, I had a good laugh. The audience was scattered throughout the room, huddled under umbrellas.

During the levitation act, Roberta, one of our cast members, was subjected to something on the order of water boarding. As she floated up, a new leak sprang up, (Or should I say sprang down?) over the stage area. The water dripped all over her face, and by the end of the illusion she was thoroughly waterlogged. Her mascara had run, her hair was soaked, and she appeared ready to confess any state secret that might have been demanded of her.

None of this kept the audience from responding enthusiastically, however. Maybe they thought we did this every show.

Ray Winder Remembers

Ray Winder began his career in show biz in the 1950s with Wyman Baker, a ghost show operator. For anyone too young to remember, the ghost shows were spooky-themed magic shows that would be presented in movie theaters before a horror film, usually around midnight.

As a general rule, the ghost shows did not use phone rooms. They marketed themselves in much the same fashion that movies did, but by 1972 when he joined Bill English, they had become a thing of the past. Even though Ray did not have much experience in phone promoting, he managed to master the business within three years and headed out on his own.

Ray carried his own phone men from town to town. For the 1975 season, he assembled a unique working crew. Years later, he told me about some of the difficulties he had with this particular crew.

His main phone man was named Charles, and during the fifteen years that he worked for Ray, no one knew his real last name, possibly because he had six driver's licenses, each with a different name. Charles said that he was an ex-doctor who had lost his privileges and license, and as proof he always wore a stethoscope in his pocket, even when selling tickets in the phone room. In the course of working with him, Ray came to have some doubts about Charles' medical background, especially after he further claimed that he had once been a minister and had also worked as a CIA operative.

Little John and Big Ben had been hired straight out of prison. Ray would frequent the halfway houses and sometimes show up at the local penitentiary on release day. He only had two rules: He would never put up with anyone working when they were drunk because you can't work when you're drunk, and he would never bail anyone out of jail. And, of course, the unofficial third rule was that you had to produce sales.

Little John and Big Ben happened to belong to a slightly more exclusive subset of Ray's recruits with criminal records. They were convicted murderers. What mattered to Ray, though, was that they could each sell several thousands of dollars of tickets each week. While Ray never minded hiring murderers, he did draw the line when it came to employing killers. He explained that murders can just happen, say over a woman, money, and or the like, but that killers were a different breed. They might kill you just for looking at them wrong. "I don't need that kind of trouble at the phone room. I have enough headaches just keeping everyone on the same page."

Case in point: Ray recalled a particular day in Columbia, South Carolina, when he had to leave the phone room to meet with the sponsors.

When he returned he found Little John on the floor of the men's room praying to a TV evangelist named Armstrong. Big Ben, who had been doing some recent drinking, grabbed Ray by the lapels and wanted to know if he would get a new body when he died; he was concerned that he might have abused his during his life. Charles then staggered in and announced in a slurred voice that he had gone to the local hospital to attend to a very special patient. He couldn't say more — it was all very secret and hush-hush. One thing about Ray Winder, whatever the situation, he knew how to either handle it or take it in stride.

He continued working phone rooms for the next thirty-eight years. He was one of the great phone promoters of this remarkable era.

The Case of the Missing Override

Among the various phone promoters who worked for our show, Cliff and Dorothy Mason stood out. They were the King and Queen of our operation, the top producers.

Bill English told me that they were always to be given special consideration. In other words, I needed to turn on the charm and bend over backwards to make them happy. If, say, they left instructions to wire transfer their overrides to them, I should make sure it happened. Normally, I did not wire money to promoters. I would get a postal money order and send it to the address left by the promoter. A wire transfer was more work for me.

Early in the 1978 tour, we had back-to-back dates promoted by the Masons. The first town was handled by Cliff, and he had grossed more than $35,000. This meant his override was $3,500. After I paid the usual outstanding bills that he'd left behind, he had around $3,000 coming to him. I had received no instructions on what to do with the override, and he hadn't shown up at the auditorium on the show day to collect it either. This was not unusual, though, because the promoters had to stay ahead of the show.

The next day I met Dorothy for the first time. She had posted a respectable gross sale for her date and was there to see the show and collect her override. After the show, I gave her both overrides and didn't give it another thought.

Several days later, Bill gave me instructions regarding Cliff's override. I then casually mentioned that I had already taken care of it by giving both overrides to Dorothy. I'm not sure how long he yelled at me, but he definitely ran up a big long distance bill that day. It seems no one had bothered to tell me that Cliff and Dorothy were going through a bitter divorce.

Later in the tour, Dorothy and I had a good laugh over this. She told me that Cliff did end up with his override, but the delay gave her valuable leverage in their negotiations. I then said something about divorce always being hard, what with the difficulty dividing up a lifetime of possessions and all that. She told me that they actually hadn't fought over the house, cars, money, or any of the other usual things. This piqued my curiosity, so I asked what the dispute had been over.

"The tap cards, of course."

It seems that they had thousands of tap cards to divide up. Every sale they had ever made was recorded on those cards, and the total came to over a million dollars. I can just imagine the lawyers' amusement at the sight of Dorothy and Cliff bickering tooth and nail over a bunch of index cards. Even in divorce, promoters were a special breed.

I need hardly add, of course, that neither snow nor rain nor heat nor gloom of divorce staid phone promoters from their appointed overrides. And Dorothy and Cliff were no exception. They went right on promoting the show, albeit separately, for the rest of that year.

Fun Phone Fact:
During the 1940s the Mills Brothers Circus developed and refined the phone room operation.

It Takes a Certain Type

This tale centers on the exploits of a phone promoter known as "Big" Bob Howard. Each year we played Nacogdoches, Texas, and he would always promote it. The town is located southeast of Dallas, near the Louisiana border, and it calls itself the "Oldest Town in Texas." The population in the 1970s was under 20,000, and a town that small, as such, would not normally have a very large gross sale.

When we rolled into town, I met with the committee at the local café. I don't recall the civic club that sponsored the show, but I do remember that I dealt with the same committee people each year. They presented the final settlement sheet with a gross sale of about $20,000. Given the size of the town population and the local economy, this was a fantastic number, and so I joked, "What did Bob do, rob the bank?" Instead of smiling, the committee peered back at me solemnly.

They all agreed they were happy with the ticket sales, but they were concerned that Big Bob had not turned in any cash. They knew of several businesses that had paid in cash, and the money had not shown up on the weekly settlement sheet.

I tried to patch things over and suggested that perhaps Mr. Howard had kept the cash and put one of his own checks in to cover it. This was the best I could come up with on short notice. I also mentioned that we would be more than happy to provide another promoter for the next year, and they agreed that that would be a good idea. I conveyed their wishes to Bill English, and the next year Big Bob was duly replaced.

When we arrived at Nacogdoches the following year, I once again made my way down to the town café. The now familiar group of sponsors greeted me, and we had a cup of coffee and exchanged pleasantries. When it came time to do the settlement, I noted that the gross sales were only $6,000. The new promoter had turned in cash each week, but the sponsor had only made $1,200 on this promotion. The year before they'd cleared over $4,000.

I could sense that all was not well. After we finished up, the treasurer leaned over to me and murmured, "We want the thief back." I nodded and said that I was sure that could be arranged.

The next year Big Bob increased the gross sales and even reported over a hundred dollars collected in cash—a peace offering to the sponsoring group. He went on to work that town for many years. As they say, sometimes it just takes a thief… to get the job done.

Upstaged

Prior to the 1990 season, Bill English dispatched me to Boston to secure a week of bookings for our upcoming tour of "The Amazing Adventures in Cartoon Land Featuring Popeye the Sailor." (Hey, we weren't doing Shakespeare here!) He had chosen the Boston area because he had an established phone promoter up there. The promoter was a somewhat mysterious fellow who went by the single name of McTavish, and he ran a permanent phone room that covered Boston and the surrounding areas. I had never booked a date in my life, so this would be a new experience for me.

At the beginning of January I settled into a hotel in Newton, Massachusetts, a town just outside of Boston, and I started calling service organizations such as the Jaycees, Lions Clubs, and Kiwanis Clubs. They represented my "A" list. Bill had already informed me that the police and firemen's fraternal organizations were sewn up tight and that I had no hope of booking them.

By the end of two weeks, I had contracted six sponsors. I had one more date to book to finish out our Boston week. At Bill's suggestion, I focused my efforts on Lowell, Massachusetts. I set up several meetings but had not made any progress until the Lions Club, I believe it was, invited me to their breakfast meeting to make my presentation.

My approach with service clubs was threefold. First, I would outline the nature of the show, part magic, part circus, part play, and totally fun for the kids. I would go on to highlight that we cast the show with the finest New York actors and the very best circus acts. I had a nice board with photos of previous productions. They could see the sets, the costumes, and all the glitter. To break the ice, I would get the club president up and do a quick magic trick. This part of the presentation would take about four minutes. I had figured out that the clubs would give you no more than fifteen minutes. Most of the time you were lucky to get ten minutes to close the deal.

The second part was pitching "the deal." For this I again relied on a large board which I placed on a tripod. It outlined and broke down the ticket sales.

Sponsor sold tickets: 50%.

Phone sold tickets: 40% to the promoter, 40% to the show, 20% to the Sponsor.

Tickets sold at the door: 50% to the Sponsor.

Example: 2000 tickets sold by the promoter @ $5 = $10,000, Sponsor share = $2,000.

200 tickets sold by the Sponsor = $1,000, Sponsor share = $500.

200 tickets sold at the door = $1,000, Sponsor share = $500.

Total Due the Sponsor: $3,000.

The board was a nice marketing piece; it focused the eye on the earning potential, and that was really all the club was interested in. Of course, no club sold any tickets themselves, and ticket sales on the night of the performance were rare. That's why I would play up the fact that the promoter would do all the work.

The last part was "the closing." I would tell the members that I was only in the area for a short time and would appreciate an up or down vote on this.

If the members had any questions, I would answer them with my stock responses. The main question was always, "Why does the show and promoter make more money than we do?" My answer would be, "Well, the promoter has to pay four to five phone people to sell the tickets, the show has eight cast members who have to be paid, and there is also the cost of moving from town to town. Your club has to supply the venue and phones. More often than not you can get this donated by someone in the town."

For this particular meeting, I could have left all my presentational materials at the hotel because, as it turned out, I didn't need them.

Before the breakfast, I met with key members of the club and outlined the program. I sensed that I had their interest and support. When the time came, I was introduced. I stepped up to the podium with my boards and my friendly smile. It was show time. Just at that moment, though, one of the club members ran into the room and called out that John Anderson, the presidential candidate, was there and would be happy to say a few words.

Before you could say "Third Party Candidate," John Anderson replaced me at the podium. Of course, if you give any politician a podium, an audience, and a few minutes, you're going to get a "Why You Should Elect Me" speech, and Mr. Anderson, hardly surprisingly, did not disappoint. He quickly filled my time and then hurried on to his next stump speech.

The meeting was now ending with everyone preparing to leave. The club president suddenly realized that I was still standing up there. He yelled out, "This guy wants to bring his play to Lowell and wants us to sponsor it. All in favor?" The room echoed yea. "Opposed?" The room was quiet. "Motion carried," said the president. And just like that, the date was booked.

I'm not sure if Congressman Anderson has any plans for making another run for the Presidency, but if he does, he's welcome to interrupt my presentations any old time he wants.

The Cop vs. The Clown

Not to be outdone by the phone promoters, the cast also regularly went that extra mile for the sake of the show, and Joy T. Clown was no exception. He was one of those performers who were always "on."

We happened to be making a late-night drive to get to the next town on our route. Normally, we would drive to the next venue in the morning, but this jump was too many miles for that, hence the night drive. I managed to stay awake until two or three o'clock in the morning. At that point I pulled over to the side of the road, exhausted, but I knew we couldn't stop. We had to make more miles that night.

Joy said he would be happy to take over. I had never let him behind the wheel before and was a little concerned about his driving skills. With few other options, though, I reluctantly handed him the keys. I then climbed into the back seat and promptly fell asleep.

I awoke to find us pulled over to the side of the road. Blue strobe lights were flashing all around us. Joy told me that he had been stopped by the local sheriff. He also told me that he would handle it.

He then rolled down the window and, as was highly typical of him, immediately launched into an explanation. He was quickly cut short, however, with a request for license and registration. In addition, the sheriff needed to see the paperwork on the trailer that we were hauling. We gathered up all the documents, and Joy handed them over. The sheriff nodded and headed back to his vehicle. Minutes passed; it seemed like the sheriff had disappeared forever. After a good twenty minutes he finally returned to our vehicle.

The conversation between Joy and the sheriff went as follows:

Sheriff: "Let me get this straight—your name is Joy T. Clown."

Joy: "Yes, sir."

Sheriff: "That's your legal name?"

Joy: "Yes, sir."

Sheriff: "What's the 'T' stand for?"

Joy: "The."

Sheriff: "Your name is Joy The Clown and you live at 349 Bogus Road?"

Joy: "Yes, sir."

Sheriff: "You're driving a car registered to a Philip Morris. Not the tobacco company, this is someone named Philip Morris?"

Joy: "Yes, sir."

Sheriff: "You're pulling a trailer owned by a Tom Lyons?"

Joy: "Yes, sir."

Sheriff: "You're licensed in the state of Georgia; the car has a North Carolina license plate, and the trailer has a Florida license plate, and they're all owned by different people. That right?"

Joy: "Yes, sir."

Sheriff: "I have you clocked at 70 in a 30 mile an hour zone. However, it would take all night to write you up and figure this all out. I want you to slow down Mr. Clown. Have a good night."

Maybe it was the just slightly manic way that Joy had in repeating "Yes, sir," but whatever it was, it was definitely too much for the sheriff. After we took off, Joy looked over at me and said he thought he had handled it rather well. I certainly couldn't disagree.

Fun Phone Fact:
CBS News recently reported that the number of cell phones worldwide has now topped 4.6 billion.

The Wizard of Odd

Each year, our tour would spend five to six weeks playing dates in Canada. We used Canadian promoters because most of our guys could not cross the border—the usual bureaucratic red tape that tends to crop up in these situations: outstanding requests to appear before a judge, arrest warrants, tax liens, delinquent child support obligations, that sort of thing. The first week always covered Toronto and the surrounding area. We were to perform at three theaters in the city of Toronto proper, and were booked and promoted by Al Stencell. Al had a lot of experience in the business, having owned and operated a highly successful tented circus in Canada for many years. The first two dates went very well. The third one ended up a little weird.

The theater was old, dark, and musty, with only a makeshift stage because it was primarily a movie house. We were very used to this kind of situation, though, and with only a little more than the usual difficulties, we managed to get the show set and ready for the evening show.

Later on, I wandered out to the lobby to check on the box office. As I was talking with Al, I noticed that all the poster boxes were covered with butcher paper. This seemed a bit peculiar, but at the same time it struck me that it was good because the small posters that we carried would stand out, for a change.

During this tour we were presenting "The Magical Land of Oz," a show that typically went over quite well because the "Wizard of Oz" story lent itself so well to the addition of magic and circus acts. We didn't have to stretch the story too much; we even had Toto too! But it may have come as something of a disappointment to at least a few of the audience members that Toto was, in reality, only a puppet.

When the theater lights went down and Dorothy entered the Land of Oz, however, we immediately saw that it would be a tough night. Our audience consisted of just one family with three kids and about a dozen men scattered throughout the rest of the theater. This was very unusual. We were presenting a family show, after all. Single men just did not come to see our shows. But, hey, this was Canada, and we were north of the border and all that.

But then, after about fifteen minutes, most of the men got up and left. We finished the show with the one family, a grand total of five people, in the theater. I should mention that the size of our audience depended upon the promoter giving out the tickets that merchants had purchased. Sometimes almost no effort was made to get the tickets distributed. Hence, an audience almost that small would not have been completely unexpected.

After the show I went to settle the box office.

This took all of thirty seconds. No tickets had been sold that night, shock and surprise! (As a rule, our show didn't end have a big day-of-show sale. Most towns only produced fifty to a hundred dollars this way.) Since we now had a little time on our hands, Al and I lingered in the lobby and cut up a few jackpots—circus lingo for stories. Meanwhile, the theater manager was working on getting ready to show the movie that was scheduled later that night, and one of his tasks was to remove the butcher paper covering the poster boxes. Once I saw the posters, the whole situation instantly became clear. Al had booked our show into a porno theater!

Perhaps the guys in the audience were waiting for Dorothy to strip and bump and grind down the yellow brick road. Even though we had some very attractive and even reasonably scantily clad cast members, apparently the show did not live up to their expectations.

The Amazing Paul Royter

Paul Royter was a Canadian, but we never held that against him. He was also an accomplished magician and hypnotist. That, of course, was a little harder to overlook. In any event, up to the year 2009, he also had one of the larger phone operations in Canada. For some reason, phone operations managed to hang on longer there.

One of his most productive booking agents went by the name of Bob, just Bob. His full name was never known to us, not that it mattered much. Bob would call Paul and tell him he had booked, say, Moose Jaw, Saskatchewan. The deal they had was pretty simple: $200 for each signed date. Paul would wire $200 and wait for the contract. A couple of weeks would go by, and he would get a signed contract for Rosetown, Saskatchewan. This seemed to occur on a regular basis.

Let me explain.

Bob was an independent booker, so, in addition to working for Paul, he booked circuses and variety shows. Every so often he would call up each of his shows and tell them that he had booked them for a particular city. In fact, he hadn't booked anything. Bob was a heavy drinker, nothing out of the ordinary there, of course, and he just needed the money to go on a bender. Fortunately, he always managed to sober up and take care of his booking duties before driving his clients like Paul completely to distraction.

But there was always the little matter that you might get a different city than the one you paid for.

Paul had a creative promoter in Calgary, Alberta, who was able to make a living through just school athletic clubs. He would sell them on sponsoring the show and then use the students as his phone people. He would come in and give them a crash course on phone sales, teaching them the art of pitching, closing, and meeting objections. He would hand them a script and then let them loose. The kids were only available after school, so this was a nighttime operation. They turned in great grosses, and they never got drunk and never stole any money.

Of course, not all promoters were all that honest. Paul told me about one guy in particular who had figured out a diabolical scheme that worked for close to twenty years. He would get a club to sponsor the show and always schedule the performance six to eight months in advance. His contract worked like this: The cost of the show would come off the top, and then he and the sponsor would split 50/50. The promotion would only take a week or two, so he could pay off the sponsor long before the show.

Months would pass, and the club members would have forgotten that they had sponsored the show. In fact, by the time that the show date came around, anyone who had bought tickets six months ago had also forgotten about the show.

If anyone showed up at the auditorium, he would cheerfully refund their money. He had to do this because he NEVER booked a show! And as for the cost of the show that he had taken off the top when he settled with the sponsoring club, that money, needless to say, remained in his little pocket as well.

Name Change

Over the course of many years, I met a good number of phone promoters, but in case of Bill Vogt, we never actually met. Bill was a top producer for our show, but he never returned to the town that he had promoted to see the show. I would send along any money that was due him, but we never managed to actually cross paths. I did, however, meet two of his phone men.

We were playing Mason City, Iowa, and it was there that I had the pleasure of making the acquaintance of these two, shall I say, individuals. They had promoted the show earlier in the month and stopped by to see the performance. The next day they were going to another town to work a "badge" deal. By way of an explanation, a badge date is when your sponsor is a fraternal police club, firefighters association, or a charity for the state police. It is usually the strongest sponsor you can have in the phone promotion business. Are you going to say "No" to your local police when they call and ask you to support their charity? Many times the charities supported the widows of slain officers. "Well, it's technically part of their job. Don't we pay taxes to cover that stuff?" This kind of a response, it goes without saying, won't do much to get you on the good side of the law.

They introduced themselves as Mr. Smith and Mr. Jones. I was sure that this could not be their real names, come on, Smith and Jones? I jokingly mentioned that they could have come up with better aliases, but they assured me that these were their real names and produced their driver licenses to prove it.

This is where truth gets stranger than fiction. The names on their licenses read as follows: Lieutenant Smith and Captain Jones. I did a double take and posed the reasonable question to both of them. Is this for real? It turns out that both of them had worked badge deals for many years, and in the phone promotion business the first order of business is to get the caller's attention. If Joe Smith calls you and is representing the Fraternal Order of Police, well, that's one thing. If Lieutenant Smith is calling you from the Fraternal Order of Police, then that's something else altogether.

It seems that these two geniuses had figured out that it wasn't all that hard to get your name changed legally. Fill out a few forms, pay a few fees, and bingo, you're somebody new. And it goes without saying that these particular name choices worked like magic for sponsoring organizations that happened to be filled with captains and lieutenants. They didn't get many people hanging up on their calls.

I had to admit that they certainly deserved credit for being so fully committed to this crazy business. Even I wouldn't change my name for a few extra dollars. But then again, if the bucks are big enough, you just might see Mike Exxon on stage the next time I come to your town.

Prospecting For Gold

Howard Cameron was a gold prospector and a part-time phone promoter. He spent five months each year working the streams around Idaho and Montana searching for gold. The rest of the time, he would run phone rooms for Bill English. Unfortunately for the show's bottom line, he often proved to be a better gold prospector than phone promoter. On many occasions, he would enthusiastically show us some of his big finds. I remember one nugget that was quite large, pretty impressive, especially for a phone promoter. His gross sales, however, were usually a bit less impressive.

In 1979 he was assigned to promote Butte, Montana. We'd heard that our local sponsor was the Lions Club, and with Howard doing the promoting, our hopes were not high for date's grosses. It was clear from the beginning that Butte was not going to win our highest-grossing-town-on-the-tour award.

Our accommodations in Butte didn't put us in much of an optimistic mood either. We rolled into town on show day, and the difficulties started almost immediately. We never made motel reservations in advance, the reason being that Phil Morris would not pop for a credit card or authorize money to be spent on making reservations. This time the only hotel I could find was downtown, and it doubled as a homeless shelter. It dated from when Butte was a thriving mining town, but unfortunately that heyday happened to have been in the 1880s. In other words, the joint was over a hundred years old. The rooms did not even have bathrooms — we had to walk down the hall to them. The clerk handed me six skeleton keys to get into our rooms, and when my cast saw what they were in for, they were far from pleased. All I could say to them was that I was staying there too.

We then headed down to the auditorium at the local high school. It was your standard 1920s school auditorium with close to 1000 seats.

Howard soon showed up, looking as happy as an alcoholic with a full bottle of bourbon. Come to think of it, he did have a taste for bourbon, but in any event, there was certainly no mistaking his mood that day. In a rather loud and dramatic voice he exclaimed, "Michael, my boy, I've hit gold. Pure GOLD!" Of course, I imagined that he had found the Lost Dutchman's Mine or some other treasure. This time, though, it had nothing to do with nuggets. He handed me the recap sheet, and, shockingly, the sales were more than $7,000, (which meant that the real sales had to have been more than $10,000.)

"This is excellent Howard, how did you get so lucky?" I inquired.

"It had nothing to do with luck, my boy. It's my new pitch. It's pure gold. Golden, I tell you!" He gave me a copy of the pitch that his salesmen had read over the phone, and I could immediately see why it had worked so well. It was 1979, well before Congress passed the Americans with Disabilities Act. Here's the pitch:

Hi, is Mr./Mrs._____, the owner, available?

Good morning/afternoon Mr. / Mrs. _____ this is Mike Jones (enter your favorite alias here) calling for your local Lions Club.

PAUSE
(Rule #1—Never, never pause in a pitch; the owner will tell you that they just purchased tickets to another local group. He brilliantly broke that rule for a good reason.)

Mr. / Mrs. Smith _____, I'm not calling to sell you tickets, we finished up that campaign several weeks ago. In fact, I'll send a runner over to your business with a dozen free tickets. You can give them out to your customers, friends, whatever. I'm calling because we are taking about twenty kids in wheelchairs to see the show next week. They are all from the handicapped home, and they don't get a chance to see a stage show too often. Some of the Lions members went down to the high school and noticed that we had a problem. We can't get the kids into the auditorium. There are steps everywhere. We are all pitching in and building a ramp for those kids. Will you help us out today with a donation to build this ramp? Can I put you down for a 2x4? A twenty-five-dollar donation would really help us out.

Howard Cameron built a lot of ramps across America that year, and they were all "pure gold."

Loose Cash

Part of my duties as the road manager was to collect the money due the show. All the settlements ended with me counting cash. No checks were accepted. So, on any given day, I might have to count three to ten thousand dollars. In addition, I had to count the unsold tickets. The unsold tickets were known as "deadwood." I have never heard a convincing explanation of the origin for this term, but it certainly deserves credit for being descriptive in its own way. I've read that it was used by writers and publishers to refer to padding a book with extra pages of superfluous text, but then again, perhaps it all started with stage coach drivers counting passengers en route to Deadwood, South Dakota. Maybe the simplest explanation is that tickets are made of heavy cardboard which is simply a dead tree product. Who knows?

The tickets were easy to count. After several years of practice, I could pick up a stack of tickets, riffle the ends and do a fast count. I could count a hundred tickets in less than five seconds. Years later, I had a standing arrangement with Rex Post, the road manager of the Harlem Globetrotters, if my count was off by more than three tickets, I would owe him a dinner. I never did buy Rex a meal.

The cash count was different. I never had a cash counter. Every bank in America has them but, I never saw one. Every dollar was counted by hand—my hands. Some days it would take hours.

I went to a local bank each day to transfer money to the home office. This would involve walking into the bank and filling out a wire transfer form. Today, with the drug and money laundering laws, this would be impossible. Everything was carried in an old beat-up leather briefcase. This bag went everywhere with me. If we stopped at a restaurant, it went with me. If we stopped at a roadside restroom, it went into the bathroom with me. It was like the briefcase that follows the President with the nuclear launch codes.

During the weekends, I would collect a lot of cash; I would have three days worth of settlement money in the briefcase. This tale concerns one particular weekend. It was the Fourth of July weekend, and of course, the banks were closed. So I ended up with close to twenty thousand dollars in my briefcase. In fact, there was so much money that it filled the whole thing.

Now I'm a strong believer that our country's independence requires celebrating. In fact, I'm sure I raised a few glasses to toast our freedom. It may have been more than a few.

Tuesday morning was very foggy. Meteorologically speaking, the morning was nice and clear. My head was where the fog was.

We had an early morning jump to the next town. I checked us out of our mom and pop hotel, and we headed down the road.

We had traveled about thirty miles when I decided to stop and get some gas. I was also in need of hot coffee to help lift the haze.

I went to pay for the gas, and that was when the panic hit me. It was that feeling that I'm sure everyone has had at one time or another. It starts in your gut, and suddenly it feels like your stomach is in an elevator plummeting toward the ground floor. My mind was reeling as my alarm increased. I did not have my briefcase!

I don't remember much about the trip back to the hotel. I'm sure I broke at least a few speed limits along the way.

I pulled into the hotel and ran to the office. The owners were there and they looked like they had seen a ghost. My briefcase was sitting on the check-in counter. They pushed the briefcase toward me and said, "Here, take your briefcase. It's all there. We don't want no trouble."

Obviously, they had opened it and seen that it was filled with cash. No doubt they thought I was a mobster or a drug dealer. I could see real fear in their eyes. I laughed and told them the story. I wasn't a mobster; I was just in show business, but I'm not sure this did much to calm their nerves.

All the money was there, right down to the penny. Once again I found myself bemoaning

Phil Morris's refusal to invest in a cash counter as I hand-tallied every bill.

In thirty years on the road, I never lost or was short any money, but I came very close on that particular weekend. I am also ashamed to say, however, that my right to make that claim rests rather shakily on both the kindness of fate and the terror instilled in those hotel staffers by every mafia movie they'd ever seen.

Left Holding the Bag

During my touring years, I called Williamsport, Pennsylvania, my home even though I didn't actually maintain any living quarters there. I spent the majority of my time in hotels and motels across America. Still, I needed to have a permanent address, and so I rented a post office box. I could never seem to fix that place up; it had poor light and a lousy kitchen, but I called it home.

During one of our breaks in the tour, I decided to head to Williamsport and see friends and try to relax. It was during a visit with a buddy that I happened to learn that the Fraternal Order of Police was conducting a phone promotion for an upcoming concert. My friend answered the phone and immediately handed me the receiver. I guess he figured that I would know how to handle this kind of call. I listened to the pitch and offered the phone man a suggestion or two on how he might tighten up his delivery. I could sense him flipping through the stock responses they were to give if the caller voiced an objection. Critiquing the pitch was definitely not in the book. I then asked him to connect me with the person in charge.

Much to my surprise, he handed the phone to the promoter who said his name was James; typically, no last name was given. When I then told him a little of my background, he said we should get together later that night.

We both had a lot of stories to share, and I spent a few days hanging out in the phone room with James and his crew. On one particularly slow day, I challenged everyone in the phone room to a sales contest. Whoever made the next sale would get a free drink after the shift. I did have a slight advantage because I knew many of the business owners in town, and sure enough, I made the next sale, much to everyone else's chagrin.

At the end of the promotion, James asked me to do him a favor. He said he had to move on to the next town and could not stay around for the show. He asked if I could be there and make sure everything went smoothly. It seemed like a no-brainer, and he even sweetened the pot by handing me a hundred dollar bill for my troubles.

The concert featured Jeannie C. Riley. You may remember her from her big hit "Harper Valley P.T.A." What James didn't tell me was that his team had been a little loose with free tickets. If you bought an ad for the program book, they would send along two free tickets with the invoice.

The fun began when I arrived at the Shrine Auditorium. It was two hours before the scheduled show time and the stage was empty! From my years of experience, I knew the band should have been setting up by then.

I was quickly surrounded by the chief of police and several detectives. It was just like in the movies when the detective conducts an interrogation. They sat me in a theatre seat and stood over me firing off questions:

"Where is Jeannie C. Riley?"

"Where did the promoter go to?"

"Where is the money?"

"Where are the free programs?"

"Where is Jeannie C. Reilly?"

I explained that I was just there to lend a hand as a favor to James. I had no idea where he was or, for that matter, where Jeannie C. Reilly was.

The chief of police told the detectives to make sure that I stayed put. I guess you could say that I was under theatre arrest. The chief then left to make some phone calls. It was looking like they were going to try to pin the whole thing on me.

At that moment, one of the stagehands yelled that the tour bus had pulled in. Jeannie C. Reilly had finally arrived. Her manager explained that they had been delayed on the interstate because of a bad accident.

However, the problems were not over; in fact, the evening was, as they say, still young. The auditorium seated around 1200 people. At least 2000 people were outside waiting to get in to see the show. Remember all those free tickets? It seems that a lot were being redeemed that night.

I decided that I could help the police and myself at the same time. I told the chief that he needed to schedule a second show ASAP. We went to the tour bus, and Ms. Reilly was more than happy to do another show. We worked out an acceptable price, and the police handed her a check.

My plan was to admit the first 1200 patrons and get the show going. The overflow crowd would be offered a choice of waiting for the second show or receiving a refund. The good part was that they did not have to wait outside. The theatre had a large banquet hall under the auditorium. In fact, it was the same size as the theatre. It could easily hold 800 people. Most folks opted to wait for the second show.

Two problems solved and one to go. I asked the chief if he had a copy of the contract that he signed with James. As I examined it, I noticed that nowhere in the contract did it state when the program would be printed. I suggested that he track James down and discuss this with him personally. I think it was beginning to dawn on the chief that I had nothing to do with this fiasco and had actually helped them iron out a few things.

I then decided that I had helped enough and made a quick exit – stage right.

Juggle Bugging

As the owner of the show, Phil Morris did not do any phone promoting himself, but this book would certainly not be complete without at least one tale featuring him. This incident occurred in January of 1978. We were presenting "The Magical Land of Oz" that year, and Phil joined us at our first date in Muscle Shoals, Alabama. He needed to walk me through settlements with the sponsors and see how the performance was coming along.

The first run through was rough with a lot of stops and starts. The blocking had to be fine-tuned, and the illusions were new to the cast members.

Afterwards, Phil said he wanted to take me out to dinner to go over some notes he had made about the performance. This was fine by me because I had not eaten before the show. The cast had stopped at a diner on the way to the theatre, so we dropped them off at the motel.

The promoter for this date was Mary Landreu, and she had turned in a quite respectable gross. Phil always liked to take folks out to dinner, especially when business was good, so he invited her too. We headed out around 10 P.M. to find some food, but in Muscle Shoals that was easier said than done. This sleepy little town had rolled up its sidewalks, and we could not find a single place open. Phil said not to worry, though, as he pulled into the lot of a Piggly Wiggly supermarket. Mary leaned over and said she thought we were being taken to dinner. She was confused as to why we were at Piggy Wiggly. I told her I had absolutely no idea what was happening either.

Once inside, Phil grabbed a shopping cart, and we made for the produce isle. He started to go over his suggestions for the show while he pulled some products off the shelves. He occasionally asked us if we liked this item or that item. About halfway through the market, he started to tear open everything in the cart. He then began to build a mile-high sandwich and a beautiful salad. He told us to dig in.

As we stood there in the canned goods section, I think it was, we proceeded to dine. Of course, by this time of the evening anything would have tasted great to me. He told me that he had perfected this practice back when he was doing ghost shows. He called it juggle bugging. The meal was actually quite good.

The best part of the evening was when we got to the check-out. The reaction of the clerk was priceless. It was like an after-dinner show. Phil had piled up a bunch of open containers and condiments, a half empty bread wrapper, salad fixings, and the like. The clerk took one look and said "What's all this?" Phil said it was dinner and it had been good. The clerk then protested that everything was open. Phil told her that it didn't matter, that he was going to pay for it all regardless.

The clerk rang up the groceries while muttering about Northerners and how this sort of thing was not proper there in the South. It was a hoot. Of course, Phil was just ahead of his time. Today, just about every grocery store has a café or dining area.

Come to think of it, some of the more memorable meals that I have enjoyed since that particular night have been juggle bugged.

The Calculator

For this tale, I have changed the name of the promoter. He is still very much alive, and the statute of limitations may not have run out yet.

Let's call him "Vegas".

In the olden days, we prepared settlement sheets by hand. Personal computers were a rarity. So when we figured the percentages and calculations, they had to be done in our head. We had gone through an education system that actually taught you how to do these things.

However, times were changing and everyone started using hand-held calculators. It was so much faster to compute large columns of figures. This fact was certainly not lost on show people who also began to utilize this latest gadget.

Most people would look at the calculators as an aid, but Vegas saw it as an opportunity. He went out and found an engineer who could, shall we say, creatively reprogram his calculator. What he got was a device that would allow you to punch in any small set of numbers such as 2 + 2 and get a display of 4 on the screen. But if you entered 4,172 + 2,872, the screen would display 6,293.

Of course, this is not the correct answer. It should display 7,044, a difference of 751. He also had the subtraction function altered, which allowed him to offer the sponsor his calculator when they were adding up the amount of checks that were collected that week. The sponsor would think that the phone room had produced $6,293, when in fact; the promoter had sold over $7,000. Vegas would simply pocket the difference.

I was amazed that not one single sponsor ever guessed that a mistake had occurred. The first time Vegas sat down with me to settle-up, he offered me the same calculator. I told him I didn't need it because I was perfectly capable of handling large numbers in my head, and besides that, Phil Morris didn't believe in budgeting for "frills" like calculators. He then laughed and told me the whole story. I was so impressed that I told him that he simply had to come up with a name for his contraption. At the next town, he presented me with my very own "Gonkulator."

It became a cherished memento, but I made a point of never doing my taxes with it.

Postscript

I truly hope that these reminiscences have come across as loving tributes to all of the people described here whom I worked with. I have made every effort to avoid any sense whatsoever that I felt I was somehow "above" any of them because the painful, cold truth is that, for a very brief time, I was one of them.

So, in closing, let me offer you one final tale.

It might be assumed from these preceding stories that I have never actually managed any phone rooms myself, but, in fact, I did run one phone room during my twenty years with the Phillip Morris show. As it turned out, one was more than enough.

We were preparing for the 1982 season. The show was put together in Charlotte, North Carolina, where the Morris costume business was based, and then rehearsed in Richmond, Virginia. After I hired the cast, the director took charge of rehearsals, which usually left me with a certain amount of time on my hands. Being familiar with this annual routine, Bill English called and told me that they were short a promoter for Jamestown, North Dakota. He asked if I could cover this assignment and help out the show. I thought to myself, how hard could this be? I had a college degree from Lycoming College and had done advanced course work in geology and paleontology. I was confident that I was smarter than the near-derelict promoters that he tended to hire. Of course, the devil is in the details, or perhaps I should say that the devil is usually lurking whenever you think you're smarter than people who have a lot more experience in something than you do.

So I deadheaded it to Jamestown and checked into a motel. I was familiar with the town because our show played it each year. The next morning, I met with the sponsors and asked to see the phone room. They had arranged to use a rented storefront on Main Street. When I entered, my heart crashed to the floor—no phones in sight. They had all been removed. It would take six weeks to get new phones installed. I had three weeks to get this done and return for the opening of the tour.

My solution to this problem was to rent another motel room at the motel where I was staying. It had two phone lines and had probably been used as a phone room in the past. In addition, I utilized my motel room phone. This gave me three phone lines to work with.

Before I left Charlotte, I was promised that I would receive the tap cards for this town. When I called Bill, he said he would try to locate them. The cards, however, never showed up, and so I had to quickly card the entire phone book. In addition, each call we made was a cold call. We did not know any of the business owners' names and had no history of past donations.

My sponsor was a developmental home. I'm

sure that they did a wonderful job with their clients, but, unfortunately, many of the fine folks of Jamestown had never heard of them or their organization.

My gross ticket sales after three weeks were a meager $2,300. It was hard, disappointing work. Bill was kind to me; after all, I was helping the show out in a pinch. His only comment at the end of the promotion was "It's not as easy as it looks."

How true that understatement was, and the difficulties I'd had were compounded by the fact that the phone business was already beginning to slowly die off. Over the next decade new technologies like call screening and even answering machines steadily chipped away at the grosses. More and more states passed phone solicitation laws that also took their toll on the business. As a result, each year the length of the tour decreased. By 1998, my last year, we were out for only six weeks, and in each of those weeks we played only two or three cities. In other words, Bill had only about twenty towns left. When I joined the show, we had over three hundred towns.

While I was saddened to see the phone business go through this period of decline, it was still never less than a delight each and every day to tour and entertain the folks who came out to see our show. That said, though, I did see the handwriting on the wall. I started to take on other clients in 1985 and ended up working for

Johnny Cash, the Oak Ridge Boys, the Ice Capades, the Harlem Globetrotters, Kenny Rogers, and a host of other big names.

But, that's a tale for another day.

A Final Thought

It should be noted that the vast majority of phone promotions happened without incident or anything in the way of foul play. These tales very much represent the exceptions to the rule.

The innumerable phone rooms in operation during that time raised many millions of dollars for outstanding civic and service clubs. Without the phone promoters and their crews grinding out call after call, many towns would have far fewer parks, playgrounds, scholarships, and the like.

I am very proud to have contributed to this industry, and it is my sincere hope that you have enjoyed these tales.

Afterword
by
E. C. Streeter

The essence of the appeal of this wonderful memoir is, of course, the vivid portraits that Mike Straka paints of so many colorful characters. The sad truth, though, is that these types are grossly underemployed. Society does not provide nearly enough chances for them to make use of their talents, and when those opportunities do occur they tend to be far below the radar of most of us readers, unless, that is, we have the great fortune to come across a book like this one. My only regret is that Mike didn't write more because I, for one, can't get enough of his insights into this world that is closed to most of us. So here's a small attempt on my part to further contribute to the colorful-character genre:

When I was a clown on Hoxie Bros. Circus in 1975—another show that made regular use of phone promoters, by the way—the big top boss was a man named Johnnie Walker. (Needless to say, that was not his given name, and I probably don't have to mention that there was an unwritten rule on the circus lot that outlawed any inquiries into a person's original identity.) Soon after the start of the season, he managed to make his big top role almost exclusively administrative, which enabled him to devote almost all of his time to his other job of running the snack concession on the show. His executive director, if you will, the man who made sure that the big top crew did all of their jobs and frequently did the jobs of those who were either AWOL or incapacitated, was a fellow who went by the name of Stash, also a name that, in a different line of work, might have prompted a question or two.

Stash was well liked and also highly regarded in terms of his tent raising and lowering skills. He looked to be in his middle thirties with blond spiky hair and a rugged-in-a-weather-beaten-sort-of-a-way look about him. He happened to be in love with a woman named Rose who was also well into her thirties and had a somewhat similar weather-beaten look, although it didn't seem to suit her quite as well as it did him. The working men on the show all slept on bunk beds in a semi-trailer. There weren't any special accommodations for Stash and Rose that I could tell, but they seemed to manage.

One day while the big top was going up in a field outside a small town in rural Virginia, two men appeared on the lot and began making inquiries. While I don't think that they were wearing trench coats, the one memory that I've managed to hold onto is that whatever their outer garments may have been, they were almost identical. In any event, these gentlemen eventually found their way to Stash and immediately handcuffed him. It seems that for some time he'd been wanted for armed robbery.

Even though she undoubtedly missed his many appealing qualities, Rose was apparently not ready to resume single life, and so she set her sights on Harvey, the forklift operator. Sadly, Harvey's weakness for Rose's charms did not diminish his longer-term weakness for adult beverages, and a few weeks after Stash's arrest he fell off his forklift in the middle of teardown. While his drinking habit in no way distinguished him from any of the other members of the big top crew, Johnny Walker decided that the risks associated with the moving of center poles, quarter poles, and weighty stacks of seat planks were far too great to be in the hands of someone who lacked enough command of his faculties to remain upright in the vehicle he was driving.

One of the ways that Harvey's departure differed from Stash's was that he could leave with a companion of his choice, and Rose decided to take advantage of that opportunity. I never managed to find out what precisely happened to them after that; one scenario that circled back to us was that they were running a laundromat in Gibsonton, Florida. What I do know, though, is that for quite a while after their departure, Johnny Walker had to put up with some serious grumbling from the big top crew that setup and teardown were taking much longer without Harvey at the helm of the forklift.

As to Stash's fate, I'm afraid we can only guess, but thanks to *Tales from the Phone Room*, we now know that the little matter of a prison record is no hindrance whatsoever to the pursuit of a rewarding career as a phone promoter. So I would say there is absolutely no reason not to assume that he went on to live happily ever after working for a rival of "The World of Fantasy Players."

About the Author

Mike Straka is a magician and educator. He began his performing career with Circus Kirk, and, in addition to "The World of Fantasy Players," he has performed for various circuses and a host of corporate events including NBC's Christmas party and the New York Mets. He studied paleontology at Lycoming College and, in conjunction with his wife Roberta, went on to develop a series of participatory seminars on prehistory for elementary schools that they have presented over the past two decades.

Made in the USA
Middletown, DE
18 August 2018